**Helping Children See Jesus**

ISBN: 978-1-933206-82-0

# BOY AFRAID

Author: Rose-Mae Carvin
Illustrator: Sandra Jarrett, Nancy Geltmacher
Typesetting and Layout: Morgan Melton, Patricia Pope

© 2018 Bible Visuals International
PO Box 153, Akron, PA 17501-0153
Phone: (717) 859-1131
www.biblevisuals.org

All rights reserved. No part of this publication may be reproduced, stored in a retrieval system or transmitted in any form by any means, electronic, mechanical, photocopy, recording or otherwise, without the prior permission of the publisher, except as provided by USA copyright law.

## RELATED ITEMS

To access related items (such as activities, memory verse posters and translated texts) please visit our web store at shop.biblevisuals.org and enter 5080 in the search box on the page.

## FREE TEXT DOWNLOAD

To access a FREE printable copy of the teaching text (PDF format) in English or other available languages, enter S5080DL in the search box. Add the item to your cart, and use coupon code XTACSV17 at checkout. Once your order is processed you will receive an email with a link to the free download.

Psalm 139:12

The darkness and the light are both alike to Thee.

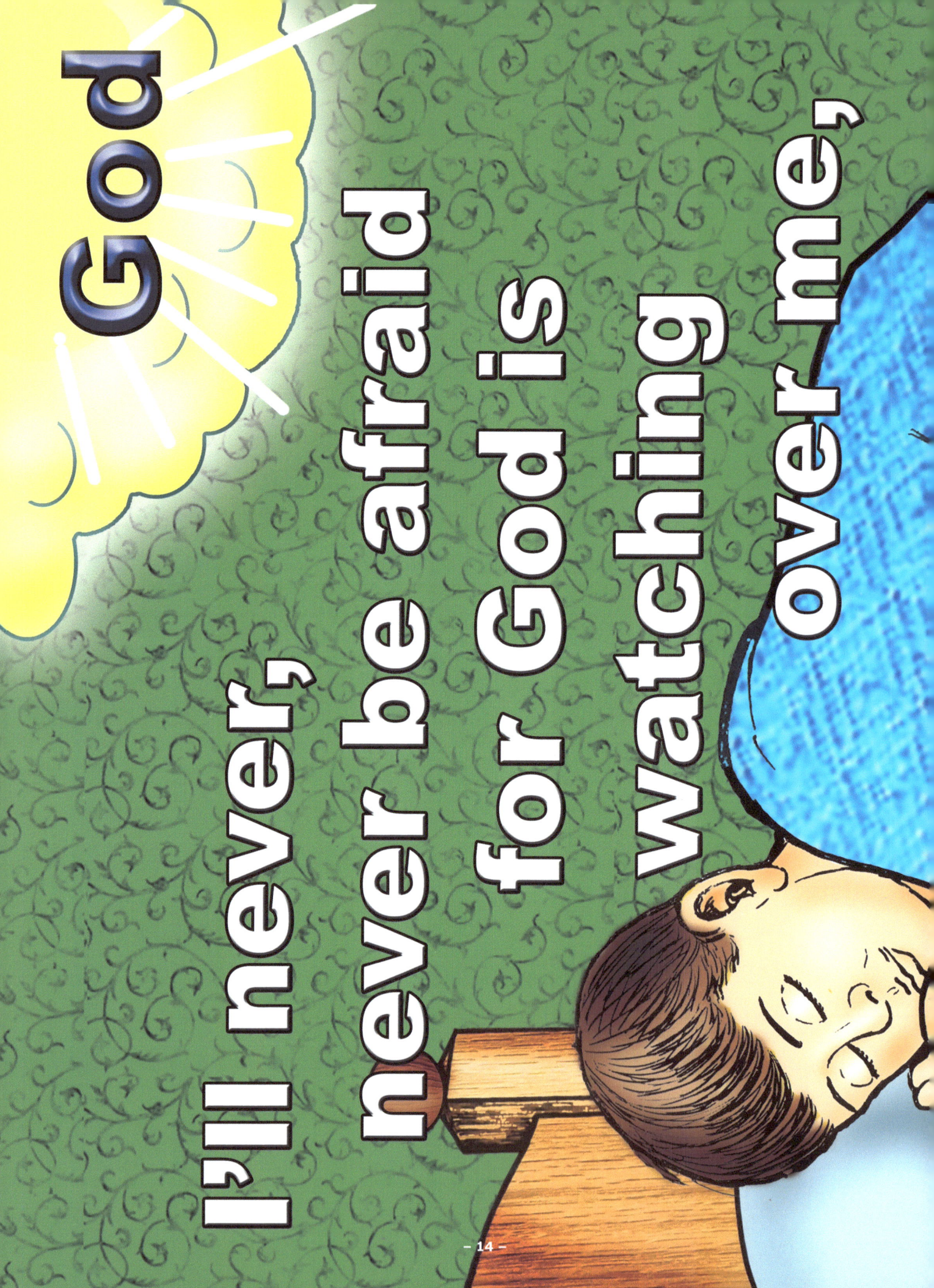

And night is just like day to Him; So I'll never be afraid.

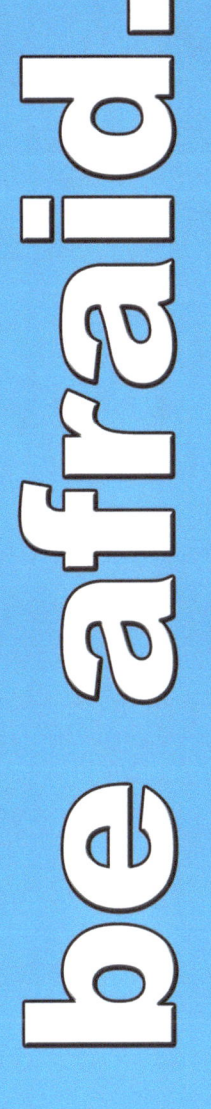
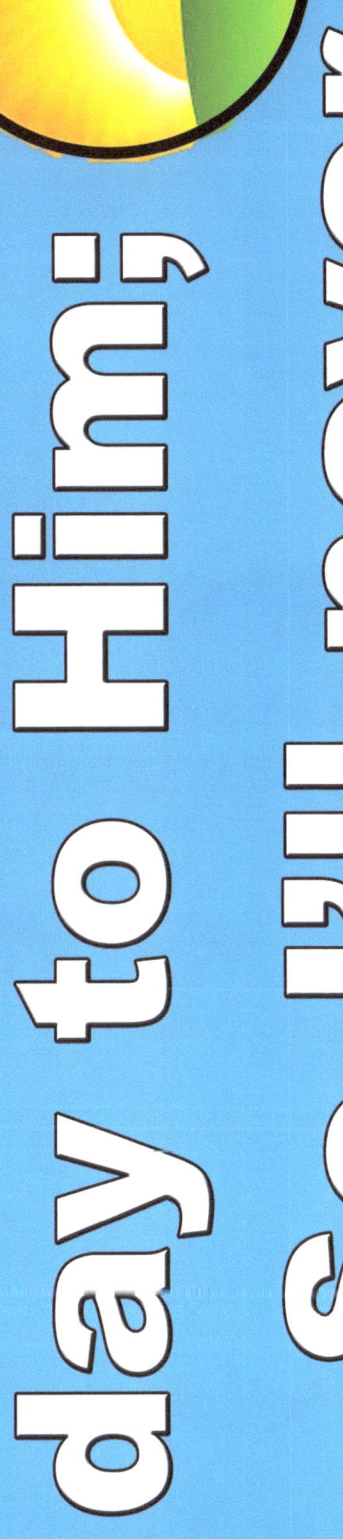
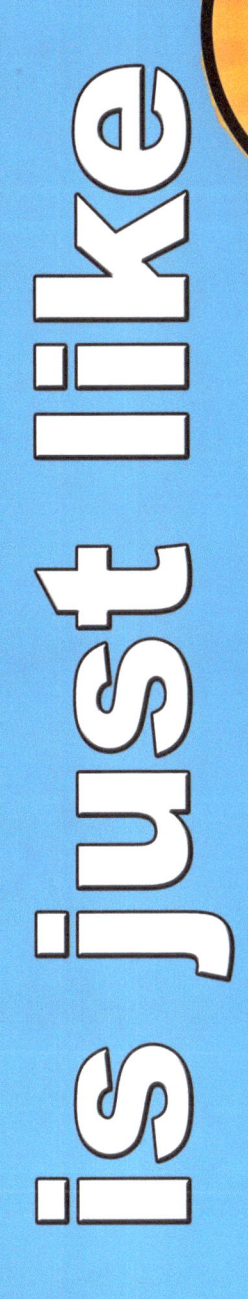

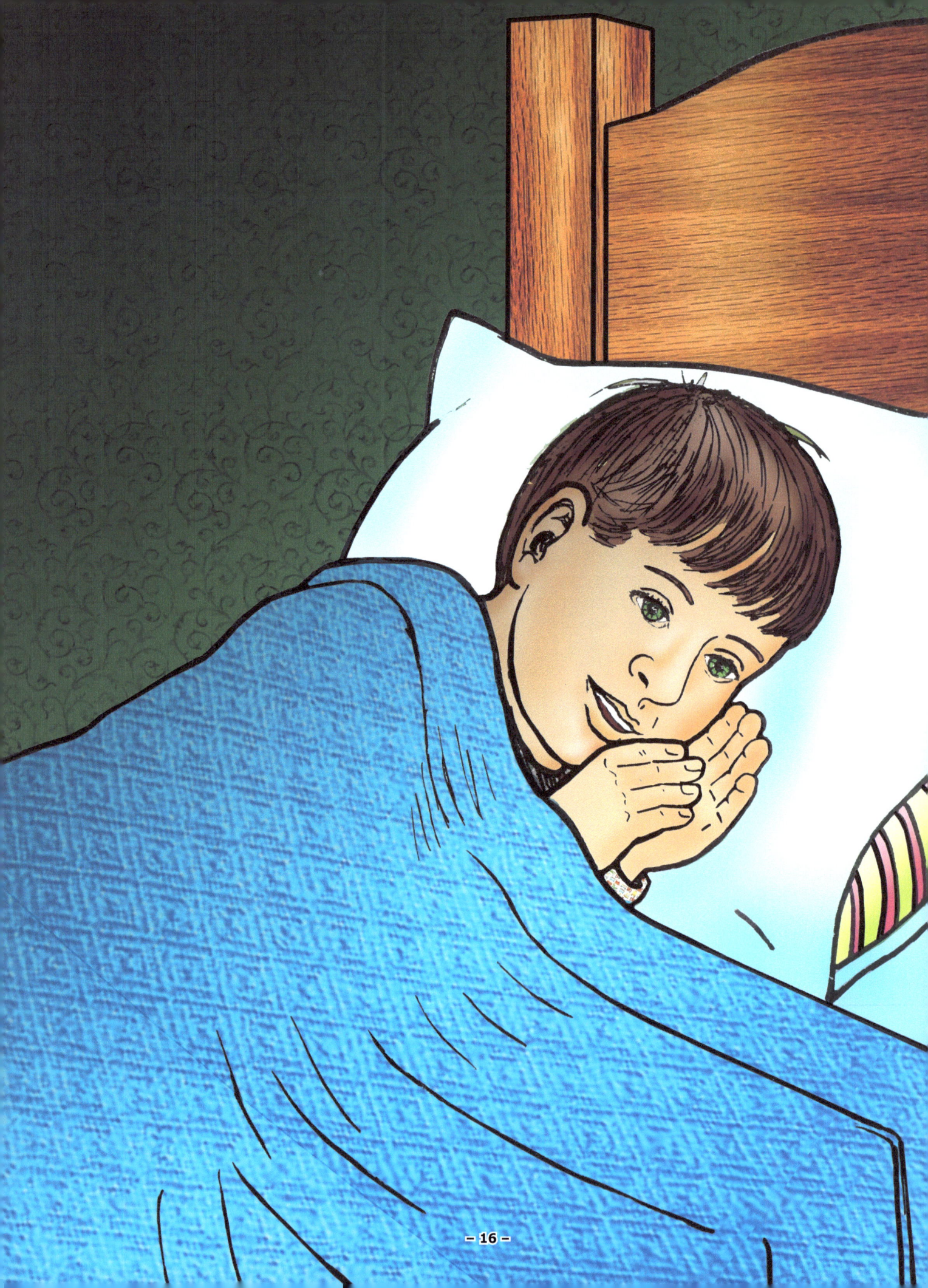

# BOY AFRAID

**Scripture to be studied:** Psalm 4:8; 91:11-12; 139:1-12; Proverbs 3:24; Matthew 18:10

There was once a boy who was afraid. He wasn't afraid of things like getting in fights. Nor was he afraid of bugs 'n snakes 'n such. Guess what! Johnnie was afraid of the dark. Yes, he was, even though he was a big six-year-old.

### Show Illustration #1

It was only when it was dark that Johnnie was afraid. He wasn't afraid of walking along streets where there were lights here and there. But then that couldn't be called *really* dark, could it? And it was this *really* dark which made Johnnie afraid. Like when he had to turn the light off in his room when he got into bed. Then the room got really dark and Johnnie was afraid.

This was the reason Johnnie tried to stay up as long as he could. Of course, most boys and girls like to stay up as long as they can–even when they are not afraid of the dark. But Johnnie was terribly afraid of darkness.

So every night when Johnnie's mother called, "John! Bedtime!" he did everything he possibly could to keep from going to bed–like taking as long as he could to put away his toys and games. Or doing a little more homework. And–when he finally had to go upstairs–he went as slowly as he could.

### Show Illustration #2

When his mother said, "Go a little faster, John," he replied, "But, Mom, I'm counting the steps."

"Well count a little faster then. And *go* a little faster, John. I'm sure you know how many steps there are."

"Yeah. But I always forget. I can't seem to remember."

Mother sighed. "Well, boy, you'd better get going–and fast. Don't forget to take your shower and brush your teeth. And be sure to say your prayers. Good night, John."

Mother shook her head, but she smiled. You see, she didn't know the real reason Johnnie went so slowly. She never guessed how terribly afraid of the darkness he was.

After at least one more trip downstairs to get a drink of water (because the water in the bathroom "tasted awful"), Johnnie finally *had* to get into his bed–in the dark.

### Show Illustration #3

He always turned down the covers, knelt beside his bed and began to pray:

"Now I lay me down to sleep,
I pray Thee, Lord, my soul to keep.
If I should . . . If I should . . ."

Johnnie choked up and trembled when he came to the words, "If I should die." You see, Johnnie was not only afraid of the dark. He was even more afraid of dying. It seemed to him the two went together.

Finally Johnnie managed to finish his prayer. Then he opened his window a little, shut his door, turned off the light and ran to his bed. Somehow Johnnie seemed to be able to find the bed, even in the dark. He knew exactly how many running steps he needed to take.

### Show Illustration #4

He made a dive under the covers, pulling them up over his head. That way he felt a little safer. But even then Johnnie would lie there a long time trembling–because he was afraid. Every night the same thing happened.

Summertime finally came and school was over until September. Johnnie went to the farm to visit his grandparents. He always liked to go there. He enjoyed wandering over the fields and helping his grandfather with the farm work. "There are many things a six-year-old boy can do on a farm," Grandfather said.

### Show Illustrations #5, 6 and 7

Things like caring for the cats and dog; getting from the cellar the potatoes and canned foods Grandmother needed; feeding the chickens and the fluffy little peeps. When he finished his chores, he could ride Lucky, Grandfather's old horse. The farm was lots of fun–in the daytime.

But nighttime came on the farm, of course, just the same as in the city. And Johnnie's room was even darker in the farmhouse, for there were no streetlights anywhere!

### Show Illustration #8

However, it always helped some because Grandmother knelt with him when he said his prayers. And she too would pray. She spoke of the Lord Jesus as her Saviour and talked to Him as her Friend. Even so, Johnnie was afraid.

**Psalm 139:12**
*. . . The darkness and the light are both alike to Thee.*

### Show Illustration #9

Somehow Grandmother knew this! She knew boys really well. One night during Bible reading time, she read some verses from the Psalms–verses which were brand new to Johnnie. (*Teacher:* If possible, please read Psalm 139:1-

– 17 –

12.) He listened to every word. His eyes flew open when she read, "'. . . The night shines as the day: the darkness and the light are both alike to Thee.' Think of that, Johnnie," she said. "God sees us in the dark exactly as well as in the light. Tonight when we pray, let's thank Him for that, shall we?"

Johnnie gave her a strange look. *Does she guess that I'm afraid of the dark?* he wondered.

Grandmother added, "By the way, instead of saying the 'Now I lay me down to sleep' prayer, would you like to say some other prayer tonight?"

Looking surprised, Johnnie answered, "I don't know any other prayer, Grandma."

"Let's talk a little," Grandmother suggested. Together they sat on the edge of the bed.

"Johnnie, do you know that the Lord Jesus died on the cross for our sins–your sins and mine?"

### Show Illustration #10

"Oh, yes, Grandma. I know He died on the cross. How could the men who nailed Him there be so cruel?"

"This is not easy to understand, Johnnie. But it was in God's plan."

"You mean God planned for Jesus to be put to death *like that*?"

"Yes, Johnnie, that's what I mean. You see, Heaven is a place where nothing wrong can enter. Yet we have all done wrong and doing wrong is sin. That means we have all sinned. You know this, don't you, Johnnie?"

Johnnie bowed his head. "Well, I'd be lying if I said I never sinned. Yes, everyone has sinned."

"Everyone but the Lord Jesus, Johnnie. He is God. Yet He became a Man. And he never sinned–never. That's why He could take our place and be punished for our sins."

"That's not fair!" Johnnie blurted out.

"Not fair, perhaps, but it is because He loves us all–loves us very much. He was not only *willing,* He *wanted* to take the punishment for all of our sins–lying, cheating, disobedience, selfishness. All our sins were laid on Him. (See Isaiah 53:6; 1 Peter 2:24.) Because He died, our sins can be forgiven. And we can be with Him in Heaven someday. He loves us and really wants us to be there. But there is one thing which makes it impossible for us to go to Heaven."

### Show Illustration #11

"Then what was the use of Jesus' dying for us?"

"Remember I said no sin can enter Heaven?"

"Yes, I remember."

"And I said Jesus died for our sins?"

"Yes."

"We can have our sins forgiven, Johnnie. First, we must truly believe that Jesus is the Son of God, and that He died for us. Then we must receive Him as our Saviour by inviting Him to live in our hearts."

"You mean that's all we have to do?"

"Yes, Johnnie. You see, God made His plan so simple that even a young boy can understand and trust Him. When we accept Him as our Saviour, we are ready for Heaven because our sins are forgiven. And this is possible because Jesus died in our place."

### Show Illustration #12

Putting her arm around him, Grandmother added, "And, Johnnie, when we take the Lord Jesus as our Saviour, we need never again be afraid of the dark–or of dying. It is the darkness of our sins that separates us from God and makes us afraid. But God is light. There is no darkness in Him. And the blood of the Lord Jesus, His Son, makes our lives clean from all sin." (See 1 John 1:5-7.)

Smiling, Grandmother added, "Johnnie, if you believe the Lord Jesus is God's Son, would you like to tell Him you believe He died for *you*? Will you receive Him by asking Him to save you from your sin? If you will, Johnnie, you need never be afraid again–not of anything, really. For then you will be a member of God's family. And He has angels to watch over and protect boys and girls who belong to Him."

Well, Johnnie may have been a boy who was afraid, but he was not a foolish boy. He was not foolish enough to refuse to accept the Lord Jesus as his Saviour. Certainly not, when he understood that Jesus had died for him–died to forgive his sins and make him ready to live in Heaven someday.

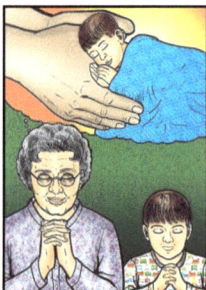

### Show Illustration #13

And so, down on their knees they went again–the boy and his grandmother. This time his prayer was different. He thanked the Lord Jesus for dying for him and asked Him to be his Saviour.

Then Grandmother prayed, "Dear Heavenly Father, help Johnnie to live exactly as You want him to live. Make him a strong Christian–with no fear in his heart. Help him to remember that he is in Your hands forever." (See John 10:28-29.) "And it is just as easy for You to watch over him in the darkness as in the light. May he never again be afraid of darkness now that he is Your child. Amen."

After their prayer time, Grandmother said, "Johnnie, I'd like to teach you a little song to sing each night when you go to bed. Would you like that?"

Johnnie's smile was big as he said, "Well, Grandma, I sure can't sing very well, but let's give it a try!"

### Show Illustration #14

Grandmother sang the song once by herself:

I'll never, never be afraid
For God is watching over me.

### Show Illustration #15

And night is just like day
  to Him,
So I'll never be afraid.

Then they sang it together several times. (*Teacher:* Have your class sing this chorus, please.)

Johnnie never forgot the little song. Every night he sang it while he was getting ready for bed. Then he shut his door, prayed at his bedside (even without Grandmother's being there!), opened his window a little, and then . . .

### Show Illustration #16

Well, then he still made a dive under the covers. But he only pulled them up to his neck–not over his head. He didn't shiver and shake with fear. Instead, he sang the little song over and over until he was fast asleep. No longer was he the *Boy Afraid*.

www.ingramcontent.com/pod-product-compliance
Lightning Source LLC
Chambersburg PA
CBHW060808090426
42736CB00002B/201